CAPTURED TELEVISION HISTORY

TV SHOWS THE WORLD FREEDOM AS THE
BERLIN WALL FALLS

An Augmented Reading Experience

T0053054

by Danielle Smith-Llera

Content Adviser: Gregory Luft
Professor, Colorado State University

COMPASS POINT BOOKS
a capstone imprint

Compass Point Books are published by Capstone Press,
1710 Roe Crest Drive, North Mankato, Minnesota 56003
www.mycapstone.com

Editorial Credits
Michelle Bisson, editor; Tracy McCabe, designer; Svetlana Zhurkin, media researcher;
Kathy McColley, production specialist; Library Consultant: Kathleen Baxter

Photo Credits
AP Photo: Lionel Cironneau, cover; Capstone Press, 23; Getty Images: AFP/DPA, 11,
AFP/Wojtek Druszcz, 49, Corbis/Owen Franken, 13, Hulton Archive, 29, ITAR-TASS/Yuri
Lizunov and Eduard Pesov, 53, Photothek/Thomas Imo, 47, ullstein bild/Lambert, 7;
Newscom: akg-images, 17, 33, 59 (bottom), akg-images/Gert Schuetz, 9, dpa/picture-
alliance, 41, dpa/picture-alliance/AND, 42, 58 (bottom), dpa/picture-alliance/Heinz-
Jürgen Göttert, 31, 58 (top), dpa/picture-alliance/Zentralbild, 43, Everett Collection,
26, Heritage Images/The Print Collector, 21, imageBROKER/Norbert Michalke, 14,
Reuters/STR/David Brauchli, 19, Reuters/Tobias Schwarz, 51, Sipa/Eclair Mondial, 38,
Sipa/Imago/Mueller, 5; Shutterstock: Everett Historical, 36, 56, ilolab, 55, Mikhail
Pogosov, 57 (left), railway fx, 57 (right), Roman Nerud, 24; Wikimedia: Ronald Reagan
Presidential Library/White House Photographic Office, 59 (top)

Library of Congress Cataloging-in-Publication Data
Cataloging-in-publication information is on file with the Library of Congress.
ISBN 978-0-7565-5826-0 (library binding)
ISBN 978-0-7565-5830-7 (paperback)
ISBN 978-0-7565-5834-5 (ebook pdf)

Download the Capstone 4D app!

- Ask an adult to download the Capstone 4D app.

- Scan the cover and stars inside the book for additional content.

When you scan a spread, you'll find fun extra stuff
to go with this book! You can also find these things
on the web at www.capstone4D.com using the
password: berlin.58260

Printed in the United States of America
PA017

TABLEOFCONTENTS

ChapterOne
WORDS AND BULLETS

When 20-year-old Chris Gueffroy left his East Berlin apartment for the last time on February 5, 1989, he faced a scary, uncertain future. But he was willing to risk everything for a better life. Hidden by darkness, he and a friend slipped through a wooded area away from East Berlin's drab, unpainted buildings toward the bright lights of West Berlin. They were determined to escape lives ruled by harsh laws. East Germany's government controlled where people lived, where they worked, and even what they said. Anyone who criticized the communist government risked brutal punishment—even death. If the friends reached West Berlin, a city controlled by West Germany, they could enjoy new freedoms. East German leaders knew that life in West Germany looked attractive. They suspected that if East Germans visited, they would never come back. So they made it nearly impossible for their citizens to get to West Germany.

Fortified walls barred the men's way with cement and steel, 300 watchtowers, and searchlights. Armed guards and attack dogs patrolled the 8- to 12-foot (13- to 19-km) walls for people like Gueffroy. East Germany forced its citizens to stay inside its borders by building the 100-mile (160-kilometer) Berlin Wall

Chris Gueffroy's photo is hung on a memorial to those killed trying to cross the wall to West Germany.

around West Berlin in 1961. Gueffroy and his friend Christian Gaudian did not have the hard-to-get documents needed to legally pass through the wall's official border crossings. But Gueffroy wanted more than a life where the government would "always decide everything for me, for all of us, from birth to death." To him, freedom was worth the risk.

If Gueffroy could get over the fearsome east side of the wall, he would see the west side covered with colorful graffiti. Much of the graffiti on the wall dividing Berlin consisted of spray-painted comments like, "The world's too small for walls." West Berliners called it the "wall of shame."

As the two men scaled the barricades with climbing hooks, alarms sounded. East German border guards aimed and fired. People living on both sides of the wall heard the gunshots. A wounded Gaudian was arrested. But Gueffroy was dead. West German news reported the brutal incident the next day, but East Germany's government refused to name the victim. Months later, Gueffroy's photograph was smuggled into West Berlin, hidden inside a box of matches carried by an elderly woman with permission to go there. West German TV could finally broadcast the face of curly-haired Gueffroy. He was the latest of an estimated 140 East Germans who had died trying to cross the wall. One of the earliest victims was 18-year-old East German Peter Fechter. The young bricklayer had been shot by border guards in 1962 and left to slowly die of his wounds at the wall, in full view of outraged witnesses.

East German guards were as determined to protect the Berlin Wall as Gueffroy had been to escape it. Harald Jaeger worked at the wall's Bornholmer Gate crossing. He carried a pistol but in his 25 years of working at the border he had never shot at an escaping East German. Still, as the son of a border guard, Jaeger believed in the wall's necessity. "When it went up on the 13th of August, 1961, I cheered," Jaeger recalled many years later. He believed in East German leader Erich Honecker,

Harold Jaeger worked as a guard at the Bornholmer Gate for 25 years and was there when it came down.

who himself had supervised the wall's construction. Honecker had called it a "victory for the forces of peace." Honecker and others feared that West Germany and its powerful allies, including the United States, could invade with tanks and soldiers. East Germany was especially troubled by having enemy territory within its borders. Both East and West Berlin were located 110 miles (177 km) inside East Germany. West Berlin was an island of democracy surrounded by a sea of communism.

East German leaders also feared invasions by dangerous ideas about freedom. West Germany's democratic government gave people choices. They voted in elections and could open private businesses. East Germany's communist government strictly limited people's choices. There was just one political party and it owned all the property and industry. But it did provide for its people. Housing and food were plain but affordable. Still, many East Germans wanted more. Karsten Klunder, one of the thousands of people who had successfully escaped, had the "urge to live in a country where I could simply do what I wanted. . . . That urge was so strong in those days that I risked my life for it."

For nearly 30 years, desperate East Germans dug tunnels, sewed hot air balloons, and strung zip lines to get past East German border guards with orders to shoot to kill escapees. Crossing the Berlin Wall without government permission was illegal in East Germany. "Your son was a criminal," security officials told Gueffroy's mother, "and that is how he was treated." Border guards who failed to stop an escape were punished, but the border guards who killed Gueffroy received a reward. Still, no one imagined that Gueffroy would be the last victim of border guard bullets—or that nine months after his death, border guards would themselves fear for their lives.

Fast forward to November 9, 1989, a normal day on duty at the Berlin Wall—quiet and boring.

"[I had] the urge to live in a country where I could simply do what I wanted. . . . That urge was so strong in those days that I risked my life for it."

WAKING UP TO THE WALL

Construction of the Berlin Wall began in 1961 at the Brandenburg Gate.

East Germany's communist government promised to provide for all the needs of hard-working citizens. But it was not a carefree worker's paradise. The government owned all of the country's farms, factories, and businesses. That meant that all East Germans worked for the government and had to follow its rules. West Germans, on the other hand, could work for private businesses or even open their own. East Germans could not even disagree with the government's communist ideology without risking prison, exile, or even execution. West Germans could choose what to believe from a variety of opinions expressed on radio, newspapers, films, and on TV.

For years after the end of World War II in 1945, a flood of East Germans poured into West Germany across the 850-mile (1368-km) border until East Germany closed it in 1952. Yet traffic between East and West Berlin still offered East Germans a way to escape west. Residents of East and West Berlin were allowed to cross over to go to work, visit family, or shop. But each day 2,000 East Germans traveled into West Germany across the Berlin border to live. By 1961 East Germany had lost 20 percent of its population. East Germany's government took a drastic step to stop the loss of its workforce.

Residents of both East and West Berlin awoke to a surprise on Sunday morning, August 13, 1961: workers digging holes and breaking up sidewalks. A barbed-wire barricade would soon follow along the border between the two countries. Armed soldiers made sure no one escaped across the border, including those building the wall. Less than two weeks later, border guards shot and killed their first would-be escapee, 24-year-old Gunter Litfin.

Work on the wall would go on for decades. More cement and steel built the walls thicker and taller. The East German government constructed a second wall to enclose a "no man's land" made deadly by trip wires and mines. The Berlin Wall "snaked through the city like the backdrop to a nightmare," remembered radio correspondent Norman Gelb.

Border guard Harald Jaeger checked documents for the trickle of people legally crossing the border. Jaeger was usually second-in-command of the Bornholmer Gate crossing but tonight his boss was away. Jaeger was eating dinner in the complex's cafeteria at about 6 p.m. A television set was tuned to a live broadcast of an East German press conference room packed with about 300 journalists. They hoped for dramatic news. The mood in East Germany was tense. Hundreds of thousands of anti-government protesters had recently taken to the streets.

Communist Party spokesman Gunter Schabowski was simply droning through government reports. One of the journalists struggling to stay awake was U.S. television anchor Tom Brokaw. His team from NBC had built a wooden stage with floodlights for Brokaw to report any news to U.S. audiences against a backdrop of the Berlin Wall and the Brandenburg Gate. A hydraulic crane waited to lift camera operators for shots over the barricades. News about divided Berlin always grabbed world headlines. While West Germany had the U.S. as an ally, East Germany had the Soviet Union. These superpowers had faced off over the Berlin Wall for nearly half a century. And just days before, the East German government had announced it would loosen travel restrictions. But Brokaw was disappointed by the uneventful press conference and had already

The mood in East Germany was tense. Hundreds of thousands of anti-government protesters had recently taken to the streets.

Gunter Schabowski surprised the world with his announcement that East Germans would now be able to travel across the wall.

complained to a colleague, "We came all this way, and there is no real story."

Shortly before 7 p.m., as the hour-long press conference was nearly finished, the journalists jolted to attention. Schabowski was saying unimaginable words: "We have decided today to implement a regulation that allows every citizen of the German

Democratic Republic [East Germany] to leave the German Democratic Republic through any of the border crossings." Commotion broke out. An Italian journalist jumped to his feet, asking, "When does it come into effect?" Schabowski was unsure and looked down at his papers in confusion. East Germany's government did plan to ease restrictions at the wall—but only gradually. Still, Schabowski blurted out, "According to my information, immediately, without delay." Could it actually be true, the journalists wondered?

Schabowski promptly ended the press conference and squeezed past the excited journalists to the shelter of a small office. Inside, the NBC TV crew was waiting. Luckily, NBC had arranged for a private interview before anyone knew that the last five minutes of a dull press conference would change history. Brokaw and Schabowski sat facing each other as the television camera began recording their meeting for later broadcast to U.S. audiences. "Mr. Schabowski, do I understand correctly, citizens of the GDR can leave through any checkpoint that they choose for personal reasons?" Brokaw asked. "Did they have freedom to travel?" Schabowski responded, "Yes, of course." Ten minutes after he went in, Brokaw burst from the room and called out to the gathered, shocked journalists, "It's down; the wall!"

At the Bornholmer Gate, Jaeger was stunned by
Schabowski's words on TV. Just minutes after
7 p.m., Jaeger saw a worrisome sight—as many as
20 East Germans were gathered at the gate. He
thought they looked unsure of what to do. He rushed
to call superiors at the Ministry of State Security
(Stasi), the much-feared East German secret police.
Was it now possible for any East German to walk or
drive through the border gate into West Berlin?

Despite Schabowski's announcement, border
guards had received no new orders. Apparently no
one at Stasi headquarters had either. They simply
told Jaeger: "You know the order, there's nothing
new." Since Gueffroy's much-publicized death, East
Germany was eager to project a friendlier image.

Border guards and East German citizens gathered at the gate.

Border guards had orders to use their weapons only if their own lives were in danger. For now, the 46 armed guards working at the Bornholmer Gate that night outnumbered the small group of people outside the gate.

Televisions in living rooms across both East and West Germany broadcast stunning words in the following hours. Hanns-Joachim Friedrichs, the silver-haired anchor of West Germany's ARD television channel, told his viewers, "This 9th of November is a historic day. The GDR has announced that its borders are, starting immediately, open for everyone." West Berlin Mayor Walter Momper went on the air to declare that "this is the day we've been waiting for for 28 years." A West German cafe owner

"If you don't believe me, then just listen," he cried in frustration and held the telephone outside the window toward the crowd of tens of thousands.

brought East German guards gifts of coffee and wine but the guards refused the drinks.

The GDR government was in a panic. Nothing could stop the hundreds, then thousands, of people gathering at both east and west sides of the Berlin Wall. It had divided neighborhoods and even family members for more than 28 years.

Brokaw and the NBC team hustled back to their wooden stage in West Berlin. They turned on floodlights, pointed cameras at the wall with Brandenburg Gate visible beyond, and waited. Border guard Jaeger waited too. His superiors still gave him no clear instructions, despite his desperate phone calls. They even suggested he was overreacting. "If you don't believe me, then just listen," he cried in frustration and held the telephone outside the window toward the crowd of tens of thousands. His guards shouted at a West German television crew from Spiegel TV climbing fences to film the massive crowd. Shortly after 11 p.m., the crowd began to chant: "Open the gate!" Jaeger wondered what to do. What if the excited crowd turned violent? Should they open fire and defend themselves?

By 11:30 p.m., Jaeger made an historic decision. He obeyed Schabowski's words and ordered his men: "Open the barrier!" Guard Helmut Stoss pulled on the gate handles and wondered in disbelief, "Why have I been standing here for the last 20 years?"

With sweat pouring, legs trembling, and fighting tears, Jaeger realized, "I knew what I had done. I knew immediately. That's it, I thought, East Germany is finished." Spiegel TV cameras caught the moment the Berlin Wall fell. The guards stepped back as 20,000 people surged forward into West Berlin. TVs at border crossings along the wall broadcast images of cheering East Germans pouring through the Bornholmer Gate. Other gates were also opened by confused guards. By midnight, the East German government lost control of the entire Berlin Wall as hundreds of thousands rushed through. Excitement and curiosity drove many to cross the border simply to look around West Germany—forbidden for so long.

While it was early morning in Germany, back in the U.S. it was early evening and viewers on the East Coast were tuning in to the news on TV. NBC Nightly News opened with footage of the Bornholmer Gate and Brokaw announcing "The Berlin Wall can no longer contain the East German people." A satellite beamed images of Brokaw live at the wall to 14 million U.S. viewers. They saw East Germans boldly climbing the wall itself. Instead of using bullets, East German guards tried to force them off with water cannons. But, dripping and wet though they were, the people happily danced in celebration. Media historian David Culbert called the fall of the Berlin

"The Berlin Wall can no longer contain the East German people."

East and West Germans stand on top of the Brandenburg Gate in celebration on November 9.

Wall "a glorious moment for the medium of television. . . . No gifted reporter, confined to words, and no still photographer . . . could hope to compete" with television images of this peaceful revolution.

ChapterTwo
PEERING OVER THE WALL

More than 2 million East Germans poured into West Berlin during the weekend following Schabowski's Thursday press conference. They walked, rode buses, and drove identical boxy East German-made cars. But some stopped and got up close to the wall that had been off-limits for so long. Some climbed on it to dance, while others attacked it with hammers and pickaxes, earning the nickname "wall woodpeckers." People collected cement fragments as prized souvenirs. Brokaw took home a chunk of the wall to keep on his desk. It reminded him that "You can build a wall, but the people will take it down."

Crowds pulled away entire sections of the wall as stunned East German guards watched. Bulldozers and cranes soon sped up the work of making new openings in the wall. The joyous destruction of the Berlin Wall—like its frightening construction 28 years earlier—seemed to happen overnight. But a decades-long story lay behind the black-and-white newsreels of workers constructing the first wall in 1961 and the subsequent 1989 color TV images of people chipping it away.

Germans knew the story well because they had lived it. In the first crowds of celebrating East and

People were so happy about the end of the wall that they chopped pieces off for themselves.

West Germans, someone held a poster that read: "Only today is the war really over." The war they meant was World War II, which began in 1939 and ended in 1945. But the war led to the building of the Berlin Wall, which caused suffering long after

Germany lost the war. The man who started World War II was Adolf Hitler. In 1933 his Nazi Party supporters marched through Brandenburg Gate with torches when he was appointed Germany's chancellor. He took over a freely elected government, destroyed the constitution, and established himself as dictator. His ambition drove him to try to conquer the world—and make it a place only for white people. The Nazis particularly targeted Jewish people. The Nazis murdered six million Jews and many others.

Nazi Germany invaded Poland in 1939, sparking the war that divided not only Europe but the world. Germany joined forces with Italy and Japan to form the Axis Powers in 1940. Great Britain and France fought against them as the Allied Powers. Neither the USSR (Union of Soviet Socialist Republics) nor the U.S. was eager to jump into war, but the Axis Powers gave them no choice. The Nazis launched an ambitious and unexpected invasion of the USSR in June 1941. Despite massive losses, the Soviets fought on and once harsh winter weather arrived, the exhausted Nazi troops retreated. In another surprise attack, Japanese warplanes bombed the U.S. Navy base at Hawaii's Pearl Harbor on December 7, 1941. They killed 2,403 American personnel and destroyed Navy ships and planes. The U.S. and the USSR joined the Allied forces in fighting the Axis powers in battles across Europe, Asia, and North Africa.

In 1933 Germans at the Brandenburg Gate celebrated Hitler's election.

Allied powers fought Nazi Germany for years. But it was the USSR that finally ended Hitler's regime. Without the aid of Allied forces, the Soviet Army surrounded Berlin on April 16, 1945, with more than 2.5 million soldiers. More than a million shells pounded the city in a two-week battle in which 70,000 Soviet soldiers died. It was one of the deadliest battles in human history. On May 8, 1945, the Nazis surrendered. Hitler died in a bunker near the future location of the Berlin Wall.

But trouble was already brewing among the Allies, and Berlin was caught at the center. Before the Battle of Berlin, Allied leaders had met in Yalta, Ukraine, in February 1945, to plan the future of a defeated Germany. They agreed to divide up the country and its capital between them. Why then did the Soviets rush to attack Berlin alone? The USSR wanted to defeat the Axis Powers. But it also wanted to become a world superpower. And its powerful wartime ally, the United States, was its greatest competition. This competition was about to intensify.

Lines on a map divided Germany long before concrete or barbed wire. In July 1945, shortly after the fall of Berlin, victorious Allied leaders met in Potsdam, Germany. U.S. President Harry Truman, British Prime Minister Clement Attlee, and Soviet leader Joseph Stalin sat elbow-to-elbow, smiling for photographs. They broke up Germany like a jigsaw puzzle to keep that nation from ever again threatening world peace. The U.S., Great Britain, France, and the Soviet Union each took control of one piece, called a zone. Berlin, floating like an island in the middle of the Soviet zone, was also divided into four "allied occupation zones." This division also helped Germany make a new start, as the Allied victors would go on to help rebuild Germany's war-stricken zones. In a spirit of cooperation, diplomats had permission to freely cross the borders. But the USSR and its former western allies were already influencing their zones in different ways. The stage was being set for a democratic West and a communist East.

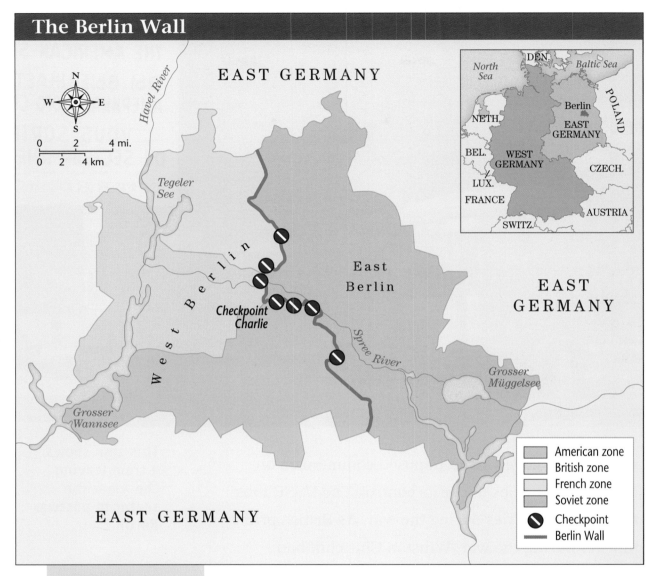

The Berlin Wall

EAST GERMANY

Havel River

N
W E
S

0   2   4 mi.
0   2   4 km

Tegeler See

West Berlin

East Berlin

Checkpoint Charlie

Spree River

Grosser Wannsee

Grosser Müggelsee

EAST GERMANY

EAST GERMANY

DEN.

North Sea

Baltic Sea

POLAND

NETH.

Berlin

EAST GERMANY

BEL.

WEST GERMANY

CZECH.

LUX.

FRANCE

AUSTRIA

SWITZ.

American zone
British zone
French zone
Soviet zone
Checkpoint
Berlin Wall

Berlin was carved into four zones after World War II.

Distrust divided the former allies too. In 1948 the USSR even refused economic aid from the U.S. Marshall Plan. This plan gave European allies billions of dollars to help rebuild their nations, bring economic stability, and support democratic governments. The USSR called the plan an excuse for western countries to control the countries it helped. Meanwhile, western countries watched with alarm

This sign shows a tram leaving the American sector in postwar Berlin.

as the Soviet government imposed communism on European countries under its control. The USSR took over many countries during the war. As British prime minister during the war, Winston Churchill had watched it happen. In a 1946 speech he warned that "an iron curtain has descended across the Continent. Behind that line lie all the capitals of the ancient states of Central and Eastern Europe. Warsaw, Berlin, Prague, Vienna, Budapest, Belgrade, Bucharest and Sofia," which, he said, "are under increasing control from Moscow" and its communist rule.

Supporting western ideas about democracy in Soviet-controlled countries was risky. Communist

To stay out of jail, avoid torture, and even to stay alive, most East Germans made sure never to appear disobedient or to criticize the state in any way.

governments took pride in providing for citizens' basic needs, but did not want them to demand freedoms enjoyed in the west. The Soviets placed Communist Party members throughout the East German government and arrested, jailed, deported, and even killed pro-democracy leaders. Through violence and fear, Soviet secret police made it a mission to wipe out pro-democracy political parties in the Eastern European countries it came to control. East Germany followed this Soviet model, raising a wall of fear to trap East Germans a decade before the actual wall of cement and steel structure was built. For 40 years, the Stasi (secret police) flooded the population of 17 million East Germans with more than 270,000 spies. To stay out of jail, avoid torture, and even to stay alive, most East Germans made sure never to appear disobedient or to criticize the state in any way. East Germans knew their apartments were watched by cameras and their telephone calls monitored. Worse still, they knew that their friends, neighbors, and even family members were often forced to spy on them.

The Soviets not only forced East Germans to regard each other with suspicion, they also persuaded East Germans to distrust the West. The Soviets took an alarming step in June 1948. They blocked all roads and railroads connecting isolated West Berlin to the rest of West Germany. For almost a year,

The Berlin airlift provided the city with fuel during the Soviet blockade.

U.S. planes dropped supplies to 3 million residents isolated by the blockade. Western powers did not give up their half of the city. In 1949 Germany was split into two countries. As the Soviet occupation zone grew increasingly hostile, Western allies combined their four separate zones into the Federal Republic of Germany (FRG). It was known as West Germany. The Soviet Union established the German Democratic Republic (GDR) in its zone but also left Soviet soldiers in place.

Divided Berlin was part of a much larger struggle between the U.S. and the Soviet Union. To protect itself and its allies, the U.S. gathered leaders from

The U.S. and the USSR raced to stockpile the most nuclear weapons.

Canada and Western Europe in Washington, D.C., to sign an agreement called the North Atlantic Treaty Organization (NATO). These countries agreed to defend each other if attacked by countries outside the alliance. The Soviet Union was alarmed by a new addition to NATO in 1955: West Germany. Suddenly, the small country had the support of a dozen allies. The Soviet Union rushed to sign a similar agreement of its own. That same year, the Soviet and Eastern European leaders—including East Germany— gathered in Warsaw, Poland, to sign the Warsaw Pact. While the Soviet Union promised to protect these allies from outsiders, its forces were also ready to crush any rebellions and keep those countries under Soviet control. With two alliances in place, the stage seemed set for a third world war. Instead, a Cold War unfolded. The U.S. and the USSR raced to stockpile the most nuclear weapons. The U.S. was thousands of miles from the Soviet Union. But when it installed nuclear weapons in West Germany in 1955, its weapons were frighteningly close to Warsaw Pact territory.

In the 1950s the superpowers learned how to mount nuclear weapons on missiles capable of traveling thousands of miles. The Cold War spread worldwide. But in Berlin, Cold War enemies were separated by just a few streets. East German leader Walter Ulbricht worried about having U.S. soldiers and weapons so close in West Berlin. But he worried as much about having opportunities for plentiful jobs and a life with more freedoms so close. Four million East Germans had already escaped west by 1961. To the world the mass migration looked like a defeat for communism and a victory for capitalism.

Longtime Soviet Premier Nikita Khrushchev believed he could convince—or even force—newly elected U.S. President John F. Kennedy to solve the problem of divided Berlin. Excited crowds greeted Khrushchev and Kennedy as they arrived for a meeting in Vienna, Austria, in early June 1961. But their first face-to-face meeting ended in hostility. The Soviet leader surprised the young new president by demanding that the U.S. withdraw from Berlin within six months. Kennedy refused and later vowed to defend "our rights in West Berlin and our commitments to its people. . . . We will at times be ready to talk, if talk will help. But we must also be ready to resist with force, if force is used upon us." Ulbricht traveled to Moscow that August and he and Khrushchev finalized a defiant plan: to close the Berlin border and "lay down an iron ring around Berlin," as Khrushchev described it. Ulbricht assured the Soviet leader, "The barbed wire has already been delivered. It can all happen very quickly."

Kennedy received news of the construction with some relief. He said a wall is "better than a war."

"We will at times be ready to talk, if talk will help. But we must also be ready to resist with force, if force is used upon us."

A WAR OF WORDS

In what became known as the Kitchen Debate, Nikita Khrushchev (left) and Richard Nixon discussed whether the U.S. or the Soviet Union was more advanced.

A fiery Cold War debate took place between leaders of the world's superpowers in July 1959. Video cameras recorded the discussion between U.S. Vice President Richard Nixon and Soviet leader Nikita Khrushchev as they toured a U.S. exhibit in Moscow, the USSR capital. It showcased a model of a new U.S.-style house, full of new technology such as a dishwasher to make modern life easier. A month earlier the Soviets had opened their own exhibition in New York City. Each leader argued that its system was best for its citizens. Khrushchev said that the communist system guaranteed all citizens government housing. Nixon countered that in the U.S. capitalist system, "We don't have one decision made at the top by one government official. This is the difference." Khrushchev replied, "On politics, we will never agree with you."

The topic of new technology fueled the spirit of competition between the two countries. Khrushchev boasted that in a few years "we'll be at the level of America, and after that we'll go farther." Nixon admitted that the race was close. "There are some instances where you may be ahead of us," he said. "For example in the development of the thrust of your rockets for the investigation of outer space. There may be some instances, for example, color television, where we're ahead of you." Behind the mostly light-hearted debate, the leaders knew that each of their countries was racing to become the most powerful nation on Earth. This "Kitchen Debate," as it was called, was televised. Television audiences saw for themselves that the Cold War was in full swing. The U.S. had built the first nuclear bomb in 1945, and the USSR built its own in 1949. By the mid-1980s, nuclear weapons in U.S. and Soviet stockpiles totaled more than 60,000.

In the race to explore space, Soviets launched *Sputnik,* the first human-made satellite, into space in 1957, and the U.S. followed with its own, *Explorer 1,* several months later. But the U.S. claimed victory in this Cold War competition by putting astronauts on the moon for the first time on July 20, 1969.

But he also called Berlin "the great testing place of Western courage and will." Just two months after construction began, the Berlin border threatened to spark world war. East Germany began blocking U.S. diplomats from entering West Berlin, breaking a promise made at Potsdam at the end of World War II. On October 27, 1961, U.S. tanks rolled forward to a border crossing nicknamed Checkpoint Charlie. Soviet tanks rolled forward to face them. Engines revved about 100 yards (91 meters) apart. For the first time, the Cold War came dangerously close to erupting into nuclear world war. After 16 hours people worldwide breathed a collective sigh of relief when the tanks retreated after negotiations between Washington, D.C., and Moscow.

At the Vienna Summit in June 1961, Khrushchev told Kennedy that Berlin was "the most dangerous place in the world." But by the end of 1961, Berlin no longer looked like the place where an international crisis would explode. Western diplomats could again freely move in and out of Berlin. Meanwhile Soviet and East German officials hoped that the wall ensured that East German citizens could not.

Yet the crisis inside Berlin was far from over for the people trapped by the wall. Kennedy reminded the world of this in a speech from West Berlin on June 26, 1963. "Freedom has many difficulties, and democracy is not perfect," he stated, "but we have

"Freedom has many difficulties, and democracy is not perfect," he stated, "but we have never had to put a wall up to keep our people in."

Speaking in Germany in 1963, President John F. Kennedy declared, in German, "I am a Berliner."

never had to put a wall up to keep our people in." He explained that the world's future was intertwined with Berlin's. "Freedom is indivisible, and when one man is enslaved, all are not free. When all are free, then we can look forward to that day when this city will be joined as one and this country and this great continent of Europe in a peaceful and hopeful globe."

ChapterThree
BROADCASTING REVOLUTION

Four years after the Berlin Wall was built, East German leader Walter Ulbricht ordered the construction of yet another massive structure. This one would be shiny, tall, and modern, built to show the West the power of East Germany and to highlight its bright future. The 368-meter (1,210-ft.) Berlin TV tower rose like a sharp weapon into the sky. It was designed to glow red, the color associated with communism.

Early television broadcasts helped drive Germany's most painful history. Hitler understood the power of broadcast words and pictures to influence people's opinions. A 1935 black-and-white documentary film of a Nazi rally—*Triumph of the Will*—used propaganda to increase Hitler's popularity. Hitler called the film an "incomparable glorification of the power and beauty of our [m]ovement." In 1935 Germany was one of the first countries in the world to begin regular television broadcasts. Nazi television official Eugen Hadamovsky saw TV's potential for delivering propaganda. He wrote to Hitler, "Now, in this hour, broadcasting is called upon to fulfill its greatest and most sacred mission: to plant the image of the Fuhrer indelibly in all German hearts."

The Leni Riefenstahl film *Olympia* was made to highlight Aryan Germans in the 1936 Olympic games.

Early developers of television also understood its power to entertain. But in the hands of the Nazi regime, even television for entertainment became propaganda. The 1936 Berlin Olympics appeared to be an opportunity for Germany to make television history: the first live broadcast of a sports event. However, the televised event was more than a sports event; it was also propaganda. Hitler hoped the success of his carefully selected white athletes would prove his racist view that they were superior to other races. He also hoped the TV footage of Germany as a gracious host of the world's athletes would distract the world from the country's plans. The cities crossed by the 1936 Olympic torch relay team—Olympia in Greece, Sofia in Bulgaria, Budapest in Hungary, and Prague in Czechoslovakia—would all be invaded by Nazi Germany within a few years.

Though World War II stalled the development of television, it also pushed it into new directions. Stations went off the air as governments pulled engineers into the war effort. But the technology that had been used to create television was used instead to entertain wounded soldiers and to help improve radar and guided missiles. And the dramatic events of war helped inspire a new, fresh approach to news. On December 7, 1941, radio stations reported that Japan, a German ally, had attacked Hawaii's Pearl Harbor. New York's new CBS TV station experimented with

"You were really hopped up and anxious and working like mad," remembered TV camera operator Robert Bendick.

an unscheduled 90-minute live TV broadcast the night of the attack. Most homes did not have TV sets in 1941, so few people saw the broadcast. For those who did see it, the broadcast was similar to the live television news watched by millions today. Station members read real-time updates on the air, showed maps, and interviewed guests who had pertinent information. "You were really hopped up and anxious and working like mad," remembered TV camera operator Robert Bendick, "and everybody was torn between the business and the horror of 'what are we getting into?' and the excitement of being in a communications medium that could bring this to the world."

Though this new television medium was exciting, Hitler had demonstrated its dangers. After the war, western powers wanted to make sure Germans were never again misled by government propaganda. After Berlin was clear of rubble, U.S., British, and French authorities established multiple radio and TV stations to broadcast a variety of opinions across the zones they controlled. After life under a dictator, German audiences needed to hear a variety of opinions. The U.S. had even passed a law in 1934 stating that television must be a place for the free exchange of ideas and opinions.

However, for the Soviets, radio and television were not tools for informing or entertaining the

Civil unrest in
East Germany
in 1953 was put
down by tanks.

public. Their purpose was to spread propaganda to
rally loyalty in citizens of the communist state. News
scripts were censored. And broadcasters, like others
in a Soviet state, risked losing their jobs, being thrown
in prison, or even executed if they criticized the
government.

Violence in East Berlin in 1953 proved the power
of uncensored western news. Construction workers
took to the streets to protest rising prices and work

Even the earliest developers of television recognized that it could help fight injustice.

demands. East German police and Soviet troops fired bullets that wounded and killed more than 100 unarmed protesters. West German radio spread the news and the next day brought larger protests in more than 250 cities around East Germany. Barry Elliott, once a director of British broadcaster BBC (British Broadcasting Corporation) in Europe, explained that broadcast journalists were not seeking "a change of regime—that wasn't part of our job—but we were stimulating the democratic process, and providing a whole range of views; by reporting strikes and demonstrations that people would not have heard about from their own media we encouraged them to come out and demonstrate."

Even the earliest developers of television recognized that it could help fight injustice. TV pioneer David Sarnoff unveiled an early television at the 1939 World's Fair and declared that TV "shines like a torch of hope in the troubled world." By the mid-1950s television would begin telling the brutal story of how Soviet states handled revolutions. In 1956 Soviet tanks and troops killed 3,000 Hungarians who revolted against Soviet control. British and U.S. TV footage of 200,000 refugees fleeing Hungary made the news feel more immediate and tragic than early newscasters simply reading a script. News footage on location became common in the 1960s as television cameras became lighter and more inexpensive.

In 1956 Austria took in Hungarian refugees who were fleeing Soviet control.

The Stasi knew the power of television and made every effort to use it. East German journalists who criticized the government put their jobs, families, and lives at great risk. The Stasi even spied on West German journalists. Ulrich Schwarz said he knew that "apartments and offices were bugged, and the secret service even recorded conversations I had with visitors in my front room. Whenever I crossed the border on Heinrichstrasse from West Berlin, I felt like I was entering enemy territory."

But the Stasi could not stop television signals. Mountains or valleys can block these signals, but

East German leader Erich Honecker called television a threat to communism, "the class enemy who comes in the evening."

the Berlin Wall could not. Television signals could even cross the Atlantic Ocean after the U.S., France, and Britain collaborated to design and launch the world's first working communication satellite in 1962. Western television now provided many choices in programs. Cultural historian Helmut Hanke, who grew up in East Germany, noted that it also provided the "only open window on the world, a window that even during the Cold War, was opened each evening in the living rooms of GDR citizens." Television was "letting in the messages of another, richer, freer world," he explained.

East German leader Erich Honecker called western television a threat to communism, "the class enemy who comes in the evening." His government sent brigades to tear west-facing antennae off roofs. A 1973 law made watching western television illegal. But it made no difference. West German TV was reaching about 70 percent of East Germany's population by 1984. Gueffroy's mother recalled that at "age 12 or 13, Chris watched political TV shows from the west and always told me that one day, he will travel to America, his dream country."

But in 1985 a remarkable change took place in Moscow. Newly elected Soviet leader Mikhail Gorbachev introduced a new, open attitude toward the west, called *glasnost* in Russian. He used television to connect with people inside and outside of the USSR. He traveled west across Europe for TV interviews. He spoke without a script and answered hard questions from foreign journalists. TV cameras even helped bridge the gap between the Cold War's archenemies. On New Year's Day 1986 U.S. networks broadcast a greeting from Gorbachev while Soviet news broadcast a greeting from U.S. President Ronald Reagan. Television also allowed leaders to confront difficult topics. Reagan stood at the Berlin Wall on June 12, 1987. In a televised speech, the president said: "We hear much from Moscow about a new policy of reform and openness. . . . if you seek peace—if you seek prosperity for the Soviet Union and Eastern Europe—if you seek liberalization, come here, to this gate! Mr. Gorbachev, open this gate! Mr. Gorbachev, tear down this wall!"

But Honecker stood firmly in the way of change. Gorbachev believed that giving people more freedom would help communism survive. Yet Honecker continued his heavy-handed rule and censorship. When Gorbachev arrived for East Germany's 40th anniversary on October 7, 1989, East German TV did not even broadcast his arrival. But East German crowds shouted, "Gorbi, help us!" Gorbachev publicly warned the unpopular Honecker that "life punishes those who come too late."

Some journalists were willing to risk their lives to bring down Honecker's government. They knew

"...if you seek peace— if you seek prosperity for the Soviet Union and Eastern Europe— if you seek liberalization, come here, to this gate!"

When Gorbachev visited East Germany, protesters held signs saying "Help us, Gorbi!"

television was a powerful weapon. On October 9, 1989, East Germans Siegbert Schefke and Aram Radomski secretly climbed a bell tower in Leipzig, East Germany, about 120 miles (190 km) from Berlin. They carried a video camera. Below, 70,000 people were chanting, "We need freedom!" Banners demanded free elections and the freedom to travel. East Germany's government barred western journalists from the city and prohibited recording the huge protest. The protest was an embarrassment for the East German government during its 40th anniversary celebration.

What would the camera in the Leipzig bell tower record? Just days before, police had arrested and bloodied protesters with batons in the same place. Now more than 600,000 East German soldiers and police waited below, armed with machine guns and tear gas.

Yet there was no violence. With the help of West German journalist Schwarz, Schefke and Radomski smuggled the video recording of the East German protest across the wall to West German television stations. East German news outlets had reported that the protesters were rowdy. Now West German television

TEARING DOWN THE WALL OF FEAR

Angry protesters destroyed Stasi headquarters a month after the Berlin Wall fell.

Less than a month after the Berlin Wall fell, East Germans once more pushed for change without bloodshed. Protesters charged into Stasi headquarters in Leipzig and officers surrendered. Hundreds stormed Berlin's Stasi headquarters in January 1990, forcing the spy network to shut down. The German government opened Stasi files to the public in 1992 and since then millions have applied to see their files. People discovered which acquaintances and family members had spied on them. They also learned how the Stasi had interfered with the course of their lives. "They worked with fear, spying on everyone, imprisoning masses of people, intimidating people, intervening in their career and preventing them from getting an education," said Stasi archive director Martin Boettger. "The archives enable you to understand these hidden methods of a dictatorship."

After reunification, German authorities put notorious Stasi director Erich Mielke on trial. The 85-year-old was sentenced to prison. The judge stated that he "will go down in history as one of the most fearsome dictators and police ministers of the 20th century."

Former Prime Minister Honecker fled first to the Soviet Union and then to Chile to avoid judgment. Finally Germany determined he was too ill to stand trial. Long after his death in 1994, his widow, Margot Honecker, remained wistful about the GDR's collapse. In a 2012 interview she said, "We just didn't have enough time to realize our plans." Instead of apologizing for the murders of escapees at the Berlin Wall, she said, "There was no need for them to climb over the wall, to pay for this stupidity with their lives." Schabowski was among the officials tried in court and sentenced for their connection to East German brutality. He later admitted that "those who died at the wall are part of the burden we inherit from our misguided attempt to free humanity from its plagues. . . . I feel guilt and shame when I think of those who died at the wall."

showed viewers on both sides of the wall the truth—the protests were peaceful. On October 16, a massive protest of 100,000 people gathered in Leipzig. East German TV news reported the event, now calling the protesters "citizens" instead of troublemakers. Even the East German government was paying attention to the story TV was telling. Honecker was replaced by new leader Egon Krenz on October 18.

The Leipzig protest grew massive. With police and the media in East Germany standing back, "Many people are picking up courage. Up to now, they dared only express themselves privately," commented one protest organizer. "Now they feel they can do it publicly." Two weeks before the Berlin Wall fell, as many as half a million protesters gathered in Leipzig, holding candles.

Brokaw and his NBC crew flew to Berlin "because it was a good story. It was this kind of percolating situation, it was simmering," he said. "And you could feel it was going to boil over." Brokaw also noticed there "was a growing feeling that the Communist Party was on the run, panicky in the face of mass migration and ever louder voices of dissent. Party officials, eager to present a warmer and friendlier image, said to us: Yes, bring your cameras into East Berlin."

Unlike East German journalists, western journalists were not intimidated by government

"Many people are picking up courage. Up to now, they dared only express themselves privately . . ."

officials. Schabowski made the announcement of the open border wall in the last minutes of the press conference on the evening of November 9th. He probably planned to leave little time for journalists' questions. The announcement had been finished so hastily that Schabowski suspected his superiors had not read the final version closely—and neither had he. "It was one of many foul-ups in those days," he later admitted.

However, the East German government did have a plan. "Our decision to allow people to travel was not a humanitarian one. It was tactical," Schabowski later explained. "We had to do something to regain popularity, and relieve the pressure." But the plan backfired. Jaeger, the border guard, later remembered that night at the Bornholmer Gate. "My world was collapsing, and I felt like I was left alone by my party and my military commanders," he recalled.

Decades after the night that destroyed the world as he'd known it, Jaeger still considered one communist leader a hero—Mikhail Gorbachev. Gorbachev won the 1990 Nobel Peace Prize for helping to improve relations between East and West. On the other hand, communist leader Honecker is remembered for his brutal efforts to keep East and West divided. In early 1989 he even declared that the "wall will be standing in 50 and even in 100 years."

Chapter Four

NEW CHANNELS

After the wall fell West Berlin's streets were swept into "the greatest street party in the history of the world," said historian Timothy Garton Ash, who was there. Meanwhile, TV networks were busy making sense of the mixture of reactions to the unfolding story. They broadcast footage of Kennedy's 1963 speech about hope for a unified Germany along with frightening footage of Nazi soldiers marching, and clips of *Triumph of the Will.*

For Germany, the peaceful fall of the Berlin Wall offered an opportunity to begin to move beyond its difficult history. On November 9, 1938, Nazi supporters roamed the streets of Berlin and other cities under Nazi control. They smashed windows and set fire to Jewish-owned homes and businesses, destroying cemeteries and synagogues and killing more than 90 people. Hitler planned to create a vast homeland populated only by white northern Europeans. The racism and violence that erupted on *Kristallnacht,* the "Night of Broken Glass," would lead to the deaths of six million Jews. Chancellor Kohl was grateful that Germany could finally celebrate a positive anniversary on November 9, the end of a revolution where, he said, "not a single window pane had been broken." The night the wall fell, he said, "We are writing a chapter in world history, once again."

Young people were a big part of the "greatest street party in history" when the wall fell.

Still, former Allied nations worried about the future. Before Germany's division, they had fought against Germany in both world wars. The day the Berlin Wall fell, television journalists in the White House were disappointed with the mood in the Oval Office. U.S. President George H.W. Bush had released a low-key public statement welcoming the "decision by East German leadership to open its borders." But as TV cameras rolled in a live broadcast, the president reclined in his chair, casually playing with a pen. "You don't seem elated," commented CBS journalist Lesley Stahl, "and I'm wondering if you're thinking of the problems."

British Prime Minister Margaret Thatcher hid her worries. She announced that November 9 was "a great day for freedom" and described watching the television coverage and seeing "the joy on people's faces." But months earlier she had privately admitted to Gorbachev, "We do not want a united Germany." She believed that the borders drawn across Germany after the war made Europe and the world more stable.

But there was no stopping the wave of revolution rolling across Eastern Europe in 1989. In fact, the changes had even started before the fall of the Wall. Citizens of Soviet states were taking charge of their governments to make changes—mostly peacefully. It was "a year of miracles," said Adam Michnik, who helped bring democracy to Poland. Free elections in June pushed Poland's Communist Party out of power. "No one took to the streets, and there were no barricades or firing squads," Michnik pointed out. In September, Hungary officially opened its border with Austria, which was not a Warsaw Pact nation. East Germans heard the news of the fall of the wall from western media and, by October, 50,000 East Germans had crossed over this new opening in the Iron Curtain.

East Germany provided the most spectacular television images. "What is freedom?" asked media historian Culbert. "We see it every time television footage of those crowds on November 9 is aired."

"No one took to the streets, and there were no barricades or firing squads."

A little girl cast a ballot for her grandmother on the day of Poland's first free elections.

NATO official Jamie Shea explained that "once people had seen the images of these popular protests on television, even in Eastern Europe, there was a feeling, 'Well we can do that too. I'm not alone, other people think like me, we are not powerless.' Modern communications, even inside the Eastern bloc, had a kind of a knock-on effect as one movement inspired others."

On November 10 Bulgarian government officials overthrew their communist leader, Todor Zhivkov, ending his 35-year rule. On November 17, 1989, protesters in Prague, Czechoslovakia, began demanding an end to their communist rule. Despite police attacks, protests attracted 200,000 people. Their communist government leaders resigned on December 29. Romania's revolution, however, triggered large-scale violence. After government troops killed hundreds of protesters, communist dictator Nicolae Ceausescu gave a speech on live TV. The crowd booed and the military turned against him. Television audiences in Romania and around the world saw images of the executed dictator and his wife broadcast on Christmas Day 1989.

Television captured the changing relationship between competing superpowers. Less than a month after the fall of the Berlin Wall, Bush and Gorbachev sat together under television lights for a historic hour-long press conference in Malta. On December 3, 1989, the leaders pledged to end the Cold War, not with a treaty but with a TV appearance. Gorbachev pointed out that "it has never been in the history that the leaders of our two countries hold a joint press conference. This is also an important symbol."

By the summer of 1990 citizens of all communist governments in Eastern Europe had held free elections to vote in new governments. The Warsaw Pact was broken. The USSR would go through its own upheaval in 1991. Gorbachev invited CNN, the 24-hour news network, to cover his resignation on December 25, 1991. Much had changed in news broadcasting since 1989. The live broadcast from Moscow would reach 150 countries at once.

What path would East Germany take after its

EAST MEETS WEST

Soon after the Berlin Wall fell, West German employers assumed East Germans would have trouble adapting to the competitive capitalist world. "People in East Germany aren't used to showing individual initiative and creativity," said the director of a West German bank in 1990. "They have no grasp of how a market economy works. They wait to be told what to do." He never imagined that one of the East Germans who crossed with the crowds at Bornholmer a year earlier would become chancellor of united Germany. Angela Merkel grew up in a forested area north of Berlin. On November 9, 1989, she was a 35-year-old living in East Berlin, returning from a sauna visit. She saw crowds heading west and followed. "There was just this incredible feeling of happiness. It was a night I'll never forget," she remembered.

Merkel's life changed quickly after that night. Though trained as a scientist, she took a job as spokeswoman for the East German government after the country's first democratic elections. She soon rose up to a leadership role. In 2005 she was the first East German, and first woman, elected German chancellor, a position she would hold multiple times—and still held in 2018. West Germany's government has three branches. The legislative body is elected by popular vote, but the chancellor is elected by the legislators. A court makes sure that Germany's executive and legislative branches follow the country's constitution.

Merkel has been called the most powerful leader in Europe. As the wealthiest and most populated country in the European Union, Germany holds strong decision-making powers among the 28 members. As a former East German, Merkel values this European alliance whose nations share one currency and whose citizens do not need to show passports to cross borders. In this spirit, she has made the controversial decision to accept floods of immigrants and refugees into Germany.

Angela Merkel and Mikhail Gorbachev at the 20th anniversary celebration of the fall of the wall.

As a 7-year-old child, Merkel saw the wall being erected, yet the experience of living for decades behind it helped her lead Germany with patience and hope. "No one knew how the Cold War would end at the time, but it did end. This is within our living experience. . . . I'm surprised at how fainthearted we sometimes are, and how quickly we lose courage," Merkel said.

revolution was a question that transfixed the world's television viewers. "I've heard many leaders speak about the German question," said Bush in Malta, "and I don't think it is the role of the United States to dictate the rapidity of change in any country. It's a matter for the people to determine themselves." Willy Brandt had an idea of what should happen. As a former mayor of West Berlin, he had watched the Berlin Wall go up. "Now what belongs together will grow together," he predicted on the day the wall fell.

Westerners watched the changes with hope and doubt. For some East Germans, doubt took the upper hand. German writer Peter Schneider explained that "many people in the GDR felt this was a catastrophe that the wall came down. . . . They were maybe fond of the coming down of the wall, but not for unification." They feared losing government-provided housing and secure jobs in state-run workplaces. They would need to learn to compete in the capitalist world of private businesses.

Desperate to survive, the communist East German government offered free elections with candidates from multiple political parties. But the ruling communist party was defeated by a coalition in the March 1990 vote. The newly elected government began discussing reuniting with West Germany. Leaders of East and West Germany signed a treaty on September 12 to erase the lines drawn across Germany at Yalta and Potsdam.

"... many people in the GDR felt this was a catastrophe that the wall came down. ... They were maybe fond of the coming down of the wall, but not for unification."

George H.W. Bush and Mikhail Gorbachev held a friendly meeting in Malta after the wall fell. They discussed the end of the Cold War.

Another vote on September 20, this time in the legislatures in both East and West Germany, proved that a majority of East and West Germans strongly favored reunification.

To unite with West Germany, East Germany would receive a valuable gift—with a catch. West Germany promised generous aid money but in exchange, East Germany had to give up everything—its government and all the property it owned. East Germany would cease to exist and become absorbed into West Germany. East Germany would even find itself part of NATO, the former enemy of the Warsaw Pact.

Another wall fell at midnight October 3, 1990, as 1 million people gathered near the Greek-style columns of Brandenburg Gate. Bullets had scarred its columns during World War II. After the war it sat deserted inside the no-man's land of the wall. That night, the crowd sang the German national anthem under the red, black, and gold flag of a united Germany. A gift from the United States, a replica of the U.S. Liberty Bell, rang out over Berlin.

Another wall, not made of concrete and steel, still divided Germans. The economic wall between east and west would be challenging to chip away. The German government and private business invested about $1.9 trillion to repair worn-out bridges, roads, and railways in the East. But reunification also brought eastern Germany a new challenge—competing with western Germany. Former West German channel ARD took over East German broadcasting in December 1990. Today the broadcasting station remains independent of the government and funded by the public. In addition to major broadcasting centers, most large businesses are located in western Germany. Just 10 percent of Germany's large companies are based in former East Germany. Since company headquarters are often in the west while their factories are in the east, eastern Germany has been called "a workbench of the west." Satellite photographs taken 25 years after reunification show that eastern Germany's lights glow more dimly than those in western Germany. "This process is not completed yet," explained economist and sociologist Uwe Blien, adding, "it's a slow one." Germans impatient for higher-paying jobs often move west.

But the former East Germany has prospered far

An international memorial for freedom was built where the wall once stood.

more than other Warsaw Pact states. Even before money and people could circulate between the two halves of Germany, television signals kept the struggling Soviet state connected to the thriving western one. "We want the citizens of both sides to know enough about each other so that they remain capable of talking to each other," explained Joachim Jauer, director of a television program popular on both sides of the wall before it fell.

Today small sections of the Berlin Wall remain—some preserved as an outdoor art gallery or forgotten in remote areas of the city. But its memory remains—even though it has now been down longer than it was up. Durs Grunbein grew up in East Germany and will never forget that he "spent one life as a hostage and one life free."

Timeline

1936

First broadcast of sports event at Berlin Olympics

November 9, 1939

In a deadly rampage called Kristallnacht, Nazi supporters destroy Jewish property through Berlin and other Nazi-controlled cities

June 26, 1953

East German construction workers begin protests that end with Soviet guns killing unarmed East Germans

May 14, 1955

Treaty signed in Warsaw, Poland, forming an alliance between the Soviet Union, Albania, Poland, Romania, Hungary, East Germany, Czechoslovakia, and Bulgaria

August 13, 1961

Construction of the Berlin Wall begins overnight

July 1945

Allied forces meet in Potsdam, Germany, to divide Germany into separate zones

June 24, 1948

USSR begins blockade of West Germany and U.S. begins airlift which ends May 12, 1949

April 4, 1949

Alliance formed between the U.S. and Belgium, Canada, Denmark, France, Great Britain, Iceland, Italy, Luxembourg, the Netherlands, Norway, and Portugal

October 27, 1961

U.S. and Soviet tanks face off at Checkpoint Charlie after U.S. diplomats are blocked from entering East Berlin

July 12, 1962

Telstar 1, the world's first communications satellite, is launched into space

Timeline

June 26, 1963

U.S. President John F. Kennedy visits West Berlin and gives famous speech supporting democracy in West Germany

1973

East Germany's government passes a law that makes watching western television illegal

September 10, 1989

Hungary opens border to Austria

October 9, 1989

Massive Leipzig, Germany, protest proceeds peacefully, a major step forward in the month-long peaceful revolution

March 11, 1985

Mikhail Gorbachev takes over control of the Soviet Union as its last leader

June 12, 1987

U.S. President Ronald Reagan urges Soviets to tear down Berlin Wall at a speech in West Berlin

November 9, 1989

The Berlin Wall falls as East German border guards allow East German citizens to cross freely

December 3, 1989

U.S. President George H.W. Bush and Soviet leader Mikhail Gorbachev meet in Malta and vow to end the Cold War

October 3, 1990

Germans celebrate the reunification of Germany

Glossary

archived—taken from a collection of historical materials

blockade—closure of an area so that people and supplies cannot enter or leave

capitalism—a system where people—not the government—own and operate a country's industry and trade for profit

censorship—limiting access to information considered inappropriate by an authority

coalition—alliance of people, groups, or countries working together toward a common goal

communism—a system where the government owns all property

dissident—a person who disagrees with the established beliefs or practices

footage—unedited recordings which can be assembled into a movie or TV show

media—ways of communicating with large groups of people such as through broadcasting, publishing, and the Internet

passport—a document issued by a government to a citizen to prove his or her nationality

propaganda—spreading information that is often untrue or exaggerated to support a leader or government

satellite—a device that revolves in Earth's orbit and, in the case of RV, receives signals from transmitters on earth and relays them to receivers on other parts of the planet

siege—a military tactic in which an army surrounds an enemy to cut off supplies and attack

treaty—a formal agreement between two countries

Additional Resources

Further Reading

Doeden, Matt. *The Berlin Wall* (You Choose: Modern History). North Mankato, Minn.: Capstone, 2014.

Marshall, George Lee. *The History of Prime Time Television*. San Diego, Calif.: Cognella Academic Publishing, 2013.

Mooney, Carla. *Asking Questions about How the News Is Created* (21st Century Skills Library: Asking Questions About Media). North Mankato, Minn.: Cherry Lake Publishing, 2015.

Richardson, Erik. *NATO, the Warsaw Pact, and the Iron Curtain* (Cold War Chronicles). Buffalo, N.Y.: Cavendish Square Publishing, 2017.

Rowell, Rebecca. *John F. Kennedy's Presidency* (Presidential Powerhouses). Minneapolis: Lerner Publications, 2017.

Internet Sites

Use FactHound to find Internet sites related to this book.
Visit *www.facthound.com*
Just type in 9780756568260 and go.

Critical Thinking Questions

How did the organization of East and West Germany's broadcasting systems reflect the basic differences between capitalism and communism?

Radio and newspapers were once the only ways for people to learn the news. How do you think adding pictures to sound changed the way audiences experienced news? How did it influence people in Germany when the Berlin Wall fell?

Many rebellions against European communist rule led to violent ends. Why do you think it was different in Germany when the wall fell?

Source Notes

p. 5, "always decide everything for me ..."Andy Eckhardt. "Victims of the Berlin Wall never forgotten." NBC News, http://www.nbcnews.com/id/6470285/ns/world_news/t/victims-berlin-wall-never-forgotten/#.WorkvRPyuiA

p. 5, "The world's too small for walls..." France and Culture. "Walls Between Peoples," http://francecanadaculture.org/en/visual-arts/events/walls-between-peoples

p. 5, "wall of shame..."John Bainbridge. "Die Mauer." *The New Yorker*, https://www.newyorker.com/magazine/1962/10/27/die-mauer

p. 6, "When it went up..." Soraya Sarhaddi Nelson. "The Man Who Disobeyed His Boss and Opened The Berlin Wall." NPR, https://www.npr.org/sections/parallels/2014/11/06/361785478/the-man-who-disobeyed-his-boss-and-opened-the-berlin-wall

p. 7, "victory for the forces of peace..." "Da Schlug's 13." German Propaganda Archive. http://research.calvin.edu/german-propaganda-archive/schlugs13.htm

p. 8, "Your son was a ..." "Victims of the Berlin Wall never forgotten"

p. 11, "We came all this way and there is no real story."... Mary Sarotte. *The Collapse: The Accidental Opening of the Berlin Wall*. New York: Basic Books, 2015.

p. 12, "Mr. Schabowski, do I under...." Gary Edgerton. *Television Histories: Shaping Collective Memory in the Media Age*. Lexington, Ky.: University Press of Kentucky, 2003.

p. 13, "You know the order..." "The Guard Who Opened the Berlin Wall: 'I Gave my People the Order–Raise the Barrier'" *Spiegel Online*. http://www.spiegel.de/international/germany/the-guard-who-opened-the-berlin-wall-i-gave-my-people-the-order-raise-the-barrier-a-660128.html

p. 14, "This 9th of November is a historic day..." Timothy Garton Ash. "The Fall of the Berlin Wall: What it Meant to Be There." *The Guardian*, https://www.theguardian.com/world/2014/nov/06/-sp-fall-berlin-wall-what-it-meant-to-be-there

p. 14, "this is the day we've been waiting for for 28 years..." "1989: A Slip of the Tongue on the Night the Berlin Wall Fell." *HuffPo*, https://www.huffingtonpost.com/laphams-quarterly/1989-a-slip-of-the-tongue_b_354122.html

p. 15, "If you don't believe me, then just listen..." "The Guard Who Opened the Berlin Wall'"

p. 15, "Open the gate!" "The Man Who Disobeyed His Boss and Opened The Berlin Wall."

p. 16, "Why have I been standing here for the last 20 years?..." *The Collapse: The Accidental Opening of the Berlin Wall*.

p. 16, "I knew what I had done..."1989: A Slip of the Tongue on the Night the Berlin Wall Fell."

p. 16, "The Berlin Wall can..." Christopher Hope. "This is What It Was Like to Witness the Fall of the Berlin Wall." *New Republic*. 18 Feb 2019. https://newrepublic.com/article/120194/witnessing-fall-berlin-wall

p. 17, "a glorious moment for the medium..." Gary Edgerton. *Television Histories: Shaping Collective Memory in the Media Age*. Lexington, KY: University Press of Kentucky, 2003.

p. 18, "You can build a wall, but the people will take it down..." "NBC's Tom Brokaw Recalls the Night the Berlin Wall Fell." MSNBC. NBCUniversal Media. March 17, 2013

p. 24, "an iron curtain has descended...." Winston Churchill. "The Sinews of Peace." Winston Churchill Society, https://www.winstonchurchill.org/resources/speeches/1946-1963-elder-statesman/the-sinews-of-peace/

p. 28, "our rights in West Berlin... " "The Cold War in Berlin." John F. Kennedy Presidential Library and Museum, https://www.jfklibrary.org/JFK/JFK-in-History/The-Cold-War-in-Berlin.aspx

p. 28, "lay down an iron ring around Berlin..." Mark Kramer. *Imposing, Maintaining, and Tearing Open the Iron Curtain: The Cold War and East-Central Europe, 1945–1989*. Lanham, Md.: Lexington Books, 2015.

p. 28, "The barbed wire has already been delivered..." Ibid.

p. 28, "a wall is better than a war..."Amy Freeman, Tim McDonnell. "Kennedy and the Berlin Wall: A Hell of a Lot Better Than a War." Wilson Center, https://www.wilsoncenter.org/event/kennedy-and-the-berlin-wall-hell-lot-better-war

p. 29, "We don't have one..."" The Kitchen Debate – Transcript." CIA.gov. https://www.cia.gov/library/readingroom/docs/1959-07-24.pdf

p. 30, "the great testing..." Thomas Putnam. "The Real Meaning of Ich Bin ein Berliner." *The Atlantic*, https://www.theatlantic.com/magazine/archive/2013/08/the-real-meaning-of-ich-bin-ein-berliner/309500/

p. 30, "the most dangerous place in the world..." Frederick Kempe. *Berlin 1961: Kennedy, Khrushchev, and the Most Dangerous Place on Earth*. New York: Berkley, 2012.

p. 31, "Freedom has many difficulties..." "The Real Meaning of Ich Bin ein Berliner."

p. 32, "incomparable glorification..." "Culture Shock." PBS, http://www.pbs.org/wgbh/cultureshock/provocations/leni/3.html

p. 32, "Now, in this hour, broadcasting ..." Mike Conway. *The Origins of Television News in America: The Visualizers of CBS in the 1940s*. Mediating American History. New York: Peter Lang Publishing Group, 2009.

p. 35, "You were really hopped up..."Ibid.

p. 37, "a change of regime..." Phillip Taylor. *Global Communications, International Affairs and the Media Since 1945*. The New International History. Abingdon, U.K.: Routledge, 1997.

p. 37, "shines like a torch of hope..." Marcy Carsey. "Father Of Broadcasting David Sarnoff." *TIME*, http://content.time.com/time/magazine/article/0,9171,989773,00.html

p. 38, "apartments and offices..." Ibid.

p. 39, "only open window on the world..." Marlis Schaum. "West German TV: The Class Enemy in the Front Room." *Deutsche Welle*, http://www.dw.com/en/west-german-tv-the-class-enemy-in-the-front-room/a-3804892

p. 39, "age 12 or 13..." Andy Eckhardt. "Victims of the Berlin Wall never forgotten." NBC.

p. 40, "We hear much from Moscow..." "Excerpts from Reagan's Talk at the Berlin Wall." *The New York Times*, http://www.nytimes.com/1987/06/13/world/excerpts-from-reagan-s-talk-at-the-berlin-wall.html

p. 40, "Gorbi, help us!..." Albert O. Hirschman. *A Propensity to Self-Subversion*. Cambridge, Mass.: Harvard University Press, 1998.

p. 40, "life punishes those who come too late..." "How 'Gorbi' Spoiled East Germany's 40th Birthday Party." *Spiegel Online*.

p. 43, "They worked with fear..." Sarah Marsh. "Stasi Files Still Cast Shadow, 20 Years After Berlin Wall Fell."

p. 44, "Many people are picking up courage..." William H. Swatos Jr. *Politics and Religion in Central and Eastern Europe: Traditions and Transitions*. Santa Barbara, Calif.: Praeger, 1994.

p. 44, "And you could feel it was going to…" "NBC's Tom Brokaw Recalls the Night the Berlin Wall Fell."

p. 45, "It was one of many foul-ups…" Geir Moulson. "Günter Schabowski, East German who Announced Berlin Wall Opening, Dies." *The Washington Post*, https://www.washingtonpost.com/world/europe/guenter-schabowski-e-german-who-announced-berlin-wall-opening-dies/2015/11/01/64d14f56-80bc-11e5-8ba6-cec48b74b2a7_story.html?utm_term=.db45d6edd6b8

p. 45, "Our decision to allow people…" "1989: A Slip of the Tongue on the Night the Berlin Wall Fell." *HuffPo*, https://www.huffingtonpost.com/laphams-quarterly/1989-a-slip-of-the-tongue_b_354122.html

p. 45, "My world was collapsing…" Erik Kirschbaum. "East German Officer who Opened Berlin Wall Wept Moments Later." *Reuters*, https://www.reuters.com/article/us-germany-wall-jaeger/east-german-officer-who-opened-berlin-wall-wept-moments-later-idUSKBN0IP2FT20141106

p. 45, "Wall will be standing in 50…" "Ten Famous Quotes About the Barrier." *The Local*, https://www.thelocal.de/20161109/ten-famous-quotes-about-the-berlin-wall-9-november-anniversary

p. 46, "not a single window pane…" *The Collapse: The Accidental Opening of the Berlin Wall.*

p. "46, We are writing a chapter…" Walter Mayr. "Winds of Change from the East: How Poland and Hungary Led the Way in 1989." 19 Feb 2018. http://www.spiegel.de/international/spiegel/winds-of-change-from-the-east-how-poland-and-hungary-led-the-way-in-1989-a-657805.html

p. 47, "You don't seem elated…" *The Collapse: The Accidental Opening of the Berlin Wall.*

p. 48, "a great day for freedom…" Margaret Thatcher. "Remarks on the Berlin Wall (fall thereof)." Margaret Thatcher Foundation, https://www.margaretthatcher.org/document/107819

p. 48, "We do not want a united Germany…." Ibid.

p. 48, "a year of miracles…" "Winds of Change from the East: How Poland and Hungary Led the Way in 1989."

p. 48, "What is freedom…" Dr. Jamie Shea. "1989: The Berlin Wall Comes Down and the Soldiers Go Home." NATO OTAN, https://www.nato.int/cps/en/natohq/opinions_135906.htm

p. 50, "it has never been in the history…." Jeremi Suri. *American Foreign Relations Since 1898: A Documentary Reader.* Hoboken, N.J.: Wiley-Blackwell, 2010.

p. 51, "People in East Germany aren't…" Ferdinand Protzman. "A Worry in West Germany: Indolence in East Germany." *The New York Times.* http://www.nytimes.com/1990/04/04/business/a-worry-in-west-germany-indolence-in-east-germany.html

p. 51, "It was a night I'll never forget…" Erik Kirschbaum. "Yearning for Freedom Brought Down Berlin Wall, Says Merkel." *Reuters*, https://www.reuters.com/article/us-germany-wall/yearning-for-freedom-brought-down-berlin-wall-says-merkel-idUSKBN0IS0PL20141108

p. 51, "As a 7-year-old child, I saw the Wall…" "Chancellor of the Free World: Angela Merkel's Journey from Daughter of a Lutheran Pastor in East Germany to de facto Leader of a Continent." *TIME,* http://time.com/time-person-of-the-year-2015-angela-merkel/

p. 52, "I've heard many leaders…" George Bush. "Remarks of the President and Soviet Chairman Gorbachev and a Question-and-Answer Session with Reporters in Malta," http://www.presidency.ucsb.edu/ws/index.php?pid=17900

p. 52, "Now what belongs…" Rick Noack. "4 Simple Lessons the World Could Learn from German Reunification." *The Washington Post*, https://www.washingtonpost.com/news/worldviews/wp/2014/11/07/4-simple-lessons-the-world-could-learn-from-german-reunification/?utm_term=.e16891d2f3e2

p. 52, "many people in the GDR felt this was a…." "Eyewitness to History: The Fall of the Berlin Wall."

p. 54, "a workbench of the west…" Ben Mauk. "Did Eastern Germany Experience an Economic Miracle?" *The New Yorker*, https://www.newyorker.com/business/currency/eastern-germany-experience-economic-miracle

p. 54, "This process is not completed…" Ben Mauk. "Did Eastern Germany Experience an Economic Miracle?" *The New Yorker*, https://www.newyorker.com/business/currency/eastern-germany-experience-economic-miracle

All Internet sites were accessed on February 19, 2018.

Select Bibliography

Conway, Mike. *The Origins of Television News in America: The Visualizers of CBS in the 1940s.* Mediating American History. New York: Peter Lang Publishing Group, 2009.

Edgerton, Gary. *Television Histories: Shaping Collective Memory in the Media Age.* Lexington, KY: University Press of Kentucky, 2003.

Gumbert, Heather. *Envisioning Socialism: Television and the Cold War in the German Democratic Republic.* Ann Arbor, Mich.: University of Michigan Press, 2014.

Hirschman, Albert O. *A Propensity to Self-Subversion.* Cambridge, Mass.: Harvard University Press, 1998.

Kempe, Frederick. *Berlin 1961: Kennedy, Khrushchev, and the Most Dangerous Place on Earth.* New York: Berkley, 2012.

Kirschbaum, Erik. "East German Officer who Opened Berlin Wall Wept Moments Later." Reuters. https://www.reuters.com/article/us-germany-wall-jaeger/east-german-officer-who-opened-berlin-wall-wept-moments-later-idUSKBN0IP2FT20141106 Accessed February 19, 2018.

Kramer, Mark. *Imposing, Maintaining, and Tearing Open the Iron Curtain: The Cold War and East-Central Europe, 1945–1989.* Lanham, Md., Lexington Books, 2015.

Sarotte, Mary. The Collapse: *The Accidental Opening of the Berlin Wall.* New York: Basic Books, 2015.

Swatos, Jr., William H. *Politics and Religion in Central and Eatern Europe: Traditions and Transitions.* Santa Barbara, Calif.: Praeger, 1994.

Taylor, Phillip. *Global Communications, International Affairs and the Media Since 1945.* The New International History. Abingdon, U.K.: Routledge, 1997.

Index

About the Author

As a teacher, Danielle Smith-Llera taught children to think and write about literature before writing books for them herself. As the spouse of a diplomat, she has enjoyed the opportunity to live in Washington, D.C., and in countries including India, Jamaica, and Romania. Her sister was an exchange student in Germany in 1989 and brought home a small chunk of the wall.